# We Believe in the HOLY SPIRIT

# We Believe in the Holy Spirit

Fr. Andrew J. Apostoli, C.F.R.

Our Sunday Visitor Publishing Division
Our Sunday Visitor, Inc.
Huntington, Indiana 46750

Our Sunday Visitor Publishing Division
Our Sunday Visitor, Inc.
200 Noll Plaza
Huntington, IN 46750

ISBN: 1-931709-31-9 (Inventory No. T18)
LCCCN: 2002107141

Cover design by Monica Haneline
Interior illustrations from OSV photo files of various paintings
Interior design by Sherri L. Hoffman
PRINTED IN THE UNITED STATES OF AMERICA

*This book is dedicated to the Blessed Virgin Mary, the Spouse of the Holy Spirit. May she assist all of us, her spiritual children, to be open to receive the renewed outpouring of the Holy Spirit that will, as Pope John Paul II has said, initiate a glorious "new springtime" in the Catholic Church.*

# TABLE OF CONTENTS

# ACKNOWLEDGMENTS

This book is not the result only of its author's writing, but also of the combined efforts of friends who assisted him in making the publication possible. The author wishes to thank in a special way two friends: Mary Majkowski who faithfully typed the text of the book, and Rene Bumb Smith who carefully edited the text for publication. The author would also like to thank all those who encouraged him to write the contents of this book, including Alan Napleton and Daniel Daou, and all those who remembered this undertaking in their prayers.

Finally, the author would like to thank Our Sunday Visitor, especially Michael Dubruiel, for accepting this book for publication.

# PREFACE

In the study of Catholic theology, we find a very important principle that links our belief and our prayer. It is simply stated: *Lex credendi, lex orandi* — "the law of believing is the law of praying." What it means is that our theological beliefs help determine and give form to our prayers. For example, since we believe that Jesus Christ is present in the Blessed Sacrament, we worship and adore Him in His Eucharistic Presence. Again, since we believe the Blessed Virgin Mary gave birth to Jesus Christ, the Second Divine Person of the Blessed Trinity, we honor her in a special way as the "Mother of God." This belief forms the basis of all Catholic devotion in honor of Our Lady.

Many of these dogmatic beliefs are found in our creeds, especially the Nicene Creed, which we recite each Sunday at Holy Mass. It contains a wonderful summary of many basic teachings of the Catholic Church. If we take the time to read and reflect on these statements of belief, we will not only grow in knowledge of the Catholic Faith, but these truths can serve as a wonderful source of prayerful reflection.

This is especially true when it comes to knowing and praying to the Holy Spirit. He has often been called the "Forgotten God." We turn in prayer much more easily to God the Father and to Jesus, Who is God's Son. By contrast, however, most Catholics pray very little to the Third Divine Person, the Holy Spirit! This is because He is not as easily known. But, despite the effort involved, it is important to come to know and love Him, pray to Him often, and be open to His guidance.

What I have done in this book is take the various beliefs in the Nicene Creed that refer to the Holy Spirit, and then offer some simple reflections for personal meditation, for private study, or for group discussion with others who want to grow in the Faith. It is hoped that these reflections will help to open up for each reader the beauty and depth of these sacred revealed truths, so that each may drink abundantly from that "fountain of living water" (cf. John 7:38) welling up interiorly in our hearts through the Holy Spirit's presence working within us.

Emphasis on the Holy Spirit is timely. Pope John Paul II has been calling each of us to participate in the work of the "new evangelization." Its goal is to proclaim Jesus Christ anew in our modern, secular, materialistic, and morally impoverished society. The pope also proclaimed the Holy Spirit to be the "Supreme Agent" and "Primary Mover" of this vital mission of the Church, and we must cooperate with Him.

Linked closely to the "new evangelization," Pope John Paul II has also frequently spoken of the "new springtime" that is about to come upon the Church and the world. He said it will consist of a great outpouring of the Holy Spirit, like a renewed Pentecost. But he has also stated that this "new springtime" will only be as effective as we are prepared to receive the Holy Spirit anew.

It is my hope and prayer, then, that God will use this book in some small way to help its readers to be that much better prepared for this new outpouring of the Holy Spirit, who is "the Lord and Giver of Life" (cf. Nicene Creed). May Our Lady, the Spouse of the Holy Spirit, also assist each reader with her prayers and maternal intercession as she prayed with and encouraged the Apostles and the other first men and women disciples of her Son, as they awaited the Spirit's coming in the Cenacle at Pentecost!

FATHER ANDREW APOSTOLI, C.F.R.
SOLEMNITY OF PENTECOST
MAY 19, 2002

# PART I

## We Believe in the Holy Spirit . . .

## 1

# Belief in the Holy Spirit Is Part of the Catholic Faith

With this reflection and those that will follow, let us focus on Who the Holy Spirit is as we know Him in our Catholic doctrine. We will use as our guide the Nicene Creed, which is recited at Mass every Sunday. There we express our Catholic belief in the Holy Spirit when we say:

> We believe in the Holy Spirit, the Lord,
> the Giver of life,
> Who proceeds from the Father and the
> Son.
> With the Father and the Son He is
> worshiped and glorified.
> He has spoken through the Prophets.

Who is the Holy Spirit? The simplest way to answer that question is to say that He is the Third Divine Person of the Blessed Trinity, along with God the Father and God the

Son. The revelation of the Holy Spirit as the Third Divine Person occurs in the New Testament. The great Eastern Father of the Church St. Gregory of Nazianzus, known as "the Theologian," tells us that the revelation of the Three Divine Persons occurred only gradually over both the Old Testament and New Testament periods:

> The Old Testament proclaimed the Father clearly, but the Son more obscurely. The New Testament revealed the Son and gave us a glimpse of the divinity of the Spirit. Now the Spirit dwells among us and grants us a clearer vision of himself.
>
> — *Catechism of the Catholic Church* (hereafter CCC), 684

In the Old Testament, there is reference to the "spirit" of God, not meaning a Divine Person, but as a quality of God, namely, His power. For example, it is said that "the Spirit of the LORD came mightily upon him [Sampson]" (Judges 14:19) and gave him the strength to overcome the Philistines. Later on when the prophet Samuel anointed young

David with a horn of oil, it is said that "the Spirit of the LORD came mightily upon David from that day forward" (1 Samuel 16:13), giving him the strength of leadership he would exercise over the Kingdom of Judah and Israel.

Other shades of meaning for the word "spirit" are related to the Hebrew word *ruah*, which can mean "spirit," "breath," and "wind" — all of which were mysterious elements for the ancient Hebrew mind. In the following reflections, we shall see how these and other Old Testament meanings prepared the way for the New Testament revelation of the Holy Spirit as the Third Divine Person of the Blessed Trinity.

# PART II

## We Believe in . . . the Lord . . .

## 2

# If the Holy Spirit Is Lord, Then He Is a Divine Person

The Nicene Creed calls the Holy Spirit "the Lord." This is a divine title. It is a way of saying that the Holy Spirit is God. This is why we call the Holy Spirit the Third Divine Person of the Blessed Trinity.

We can ask: Why did it become necessary for the Nicene Creed to state that the Holy Spirit was "Lord"? The answer goes back to the second half of the fourth century. At the time, a bishop named Macedonius was Patriarch of Constantinople, a major see in the Eastern Church. Unfortunately, he denied the divinity of the Holy Spirit. Those who followed his teaching believed that the Holy Spirit was only a creature — not divine, not God, not the Third Person of the Blessed Trinity. Interestingly, those who held this erroneous belief came to be known popularly by the Greek word *pneumatomachoi*, which literally meant "enemies [or opponents] of the Spirit."

In the year 381, the Catholic Church held its second ecumenical council to debate Macedonius's teaching. The council Fathers ended up officially condemning Macedonianism as a heresy. In 382, Pope Damasus ratified the decisions of the Council of Constantinople. This council's teaching was then added to the creed that had been formulated at the Church's very first ecumenical council held at Nicaea in 325. The Council of Nicaea had condemned the heretical teaching of a priest named Arius who taught that Jesus was not God as well as man, not divine as well as human, but only an exalted creature.

The official name of the creed is the Nicene-Constantinopolitan Creed, since it is made up of the teachings from the first two ecumenical councils. However, for purposes of simplification, it is usually just called the Nicene Creed. What was added to the creed from the Council of Constantinople strongly emphasized the divinity of the Holy Spirit.

What did the council Fathers base their teaching on? One very important argument was that when Our Lord gave His Apostles the command to baptize all who would believe, He said they must baptize "in the name of the Father and of the Son and of the Holy Spirit" (Matthew 28:19). His words put the Holy Spirit on an equal level with the Father and the Son. Since the Father and the Son were believed to be Divine Persons, didn't it follow that the Holy Spirit also had to be a Divine Person? Furthermore, the council Fathers knew that it was the special role or work of the Holy Spirit to sanctify us (make us holy) and even to "divinize" us (make us "partakers of the divine nature" — 2 Peter 1:4). But no one can make us holy unless he himself was superabundantly holy, and only God is so completely holy! Even more so, only He Who is divine can make anyone else "divine-like" or a partaker in the divine nature. It only follows that the Holy Spirit must be God. When the infallible authority of Pope Damasus confirmed this council teaching, the faithful knew it was the authentic understanding of what God had revealed and the Catholic Church taught.

# PART III

## We Believe in . . . the Giver of Life . . .

# 3

# The Spirit of Life

"The Spirit of Life" is a very appropriate title for the Holy Spirit. The close bond between the Holy Spirit, the Giver of Life, and the gift of life itself, which God has given to all His living creatures, is already indicated in the Old Testament. In our first reflection, we mentioned that the Jewish people never considered "the spirit of God" as a Divine Person, since the revelation of the mystery of the Blessed Trinity (Three Divine Persons in One God) would only come later with Jesus in the New Testament. However, they did consider "the spirit of God" as one of God's attributes or qualities, namely, His power by which He could create, inspire, or strengthen His creatures. Thus, in the first chapter of Genesis, the very beginning of the Bible, we read that the "spirit of God" (sometimes translated also as the "wind of God") passed over the formless wasteland of the earth and the darkened abyss of the sea. After the "spirit of God" passed over the lifeless void, the land came alive, teeming with vegetative life. With plants of all kinds, the earth was now able to sustain animal life and, ultimately, human life. God then filled both sea and land with an abundance of living creatures. The "spirit of God" had made creation fruitful!

The *Catechism of the Catholic Church* presents the following thought on the role of the Holy Spirit in creation. It quotes from a Morning Prayer of the Byzantine Liturgy:

> The Word of God [the Second Divine Person] and his Breath [the Third Divine Person] are at the origin of the being and life of every creature:
>
> It belongs to the Holy Spirit to rule, sanctify, and animate creation, for he is God, consubstantial with the Father and the Son. . . . Power over life pertains to the Spirit, for being God he preserves creation in the Father through the Son.
>
> — CCC, 703

This theme of the "spirit of God" as the divine creative power, the source of all life in nature, is also expressed beautifully in Psalm 104:

> "When thou takest away their breath, they die / and return to their dust" (verse 29).
>
> "When thou sendest forth thy Spirit, they are created; / and thou renewest the face of the ground" (verse 30).

The words of verse 30 (or similar versions of the words) have become part of one of the most popular prayers to the Holy Spirit. Whenever and wherever the Holy Spirit is present, there life flourishes! And because life in all its forms is a gift of God, it should be respected. Jesus Himself recognized the natural goodness of all living creatures. He even pointed out how His Heavenly Father provided for them — how He fed the birds of the air and clothed the lilies of the field (cf. Matthew 6:26-30).

St. Francis of Assisi likewise saw a great harmony among all the creatures of God. They formed, as it were, a symphony to praise their Creator, each after its own nature and qualities. He called inanimate creatures his brothers and sisters, like Brother Sun, Sister Water, and Brother Fire. Even more so did he see the living God reflected in His living creatures, like the doves that reminded him of the purity and humility of the Lord and the lamb whose gentleness called to mind the meek Lamb of God. Furthermore, he attained such holiness that he experienced a gift of peace and harmony with these creatures of God so that they were quick to respond to him, like the larks that listened when he preached to them, and the cricket who "sang" for him at his request, and the fierce wolf of Gubbio who was tamed by his words of correction.

4

# Human Life: "God Saw It Was 'Very Good' "

You may have seen the bumper sticker GOD IS PRO-LIFE. How true this is because all life, as we saw in our previous reflection, comes from God. The Church expresses this truth in her sacred Liturgy in Eucharistic Prayer III:

> Father, you are holy indeed, / and all creation rightly gives you praise. / All life, all holiness comes from you, / through your Son, Jesus Christ our Lord, / by the working of the Holy Spirit.

The high point of all natural creation is God's creation of human life, of the first man and woman, of Adam and Eve. When God made every other creature, living and nonliving, He saw that they were "good" (Genesis 1:4, 10, 12, 18, 21, 25); but after He made man and woman in His own image and likeness, "God saw everything that he had made, and behold, it was very good" (Genesis 1:31).

Here, as in the previous reflection, we see the special role of the Giver of Life indicated. Remember that the same Hebrew word, *ruah*, meant spirit, breath, and wind. There is an interplay between these different meanings in the description of the creation of Adam and Eve. We read in Genesis 2:7 that "the LORD God formed man of dust from the ground, and breathed into his nostrils the breath of life; and man became a living being." For the ancient Jewish people the very spirit (soul) in each person was a share in the breath of God Himself. The Holy Spirit is often referred to as "the breath of God."

A similar description of the role of the Spirit of Life is seen in the prophet Ezekiel's famous "vision of the dry bones" (cf. Ezekiel 37). The dry bones in the vision represented the Jewish people in exile in Babylon. They were terribly discouraged by their situation in exile from their beloved homeland. Above all, they felt that even God had abandoned them. They were about as life-filled as those dry bones! In the midst of all this, God tells Ezekiel that he will "breathe" life into them:

> "Prophesy to these bones, and say to them, O dry bones, hear the word of the LORD. . . . Behold, I will cause breath to enter you, and you shall live. And I will lay sinews upon you, and will cause flesh to come upon you, and cover you with skin, and put breath in you, and you shall live; and you shall know that I am the LORD."
>
> So I prophesied as he commanded me, and the breath came into them, and they lived, and stood upon their feet, an exceedingly great host.
>
> — Ezekiel 37:4-6, 10

These scriptural examples clearly show that there is something unique about human life among all the creatures God made. Man's soul, which is by its very nature immortal (it cannot die or cease to exist, and this is why it survives the death of the body), is a created share in God's own power of the Spirit. Furthermore, his body is destined to be "a temple of the Holy Spirit" (1 Corinthians 6:19).

As a consequence of all this, we must recognize unmistakably that every human life is sacred, from the moment of conception to the moment of natural death. If all creatures that have life reflect the living God, how much more is that true of all human beings, since only man and woman are made in God's image and likeness (cf. Genesis 1:26-27). We must always respect what the Holy Spirit, the Giver of Life, has given.

# 5

# The Holy Spirit's Greatest Work: The Incarnation

The role of the Holy Spirit as "the Giver of Life" is fully and clearly revealed only in the New Testament. It begins with His coming at the Annunciation to bring about the great mystery and gift of the Incarnation, the mystery of the Eternal Word becoming flesh in the womb of the Blessed Virgin Mary. We profess in the Nicene Creed, "[Jesus] was conceived by the Holy Spirit, and born of the Virgin Mary." The *Catechism of the Catholic Church* describes the role of the Holy Spirit in the Incarnation in these words:

> The mission of the Holy Spirit is always conjoined and ordered to that of the Son. The Holy Spirit, "the Lord, the giver of Life," is sent to sanctify the womb of the Virgin Mary and divinely fecundate it, causing her to conceive the eternal Son of the Father in a humanity drawn from her own.
>
> — CCC, 485

St. Luke's description of the Incarnation event at the Annunciation (cf. Luke 1:26-38) allows us to view it as a "new creation," the very perfection of all the works of the Spirit of Life. The passing of "the spirit of God" (His power) over the lifeless void in the "first creation" account (cf. Genesis 1:1-2) gave creation the potential to bring forth an abundance of life. How much more does the "overshadowing" of Our Lady by the Holy Spirit Himself bring about what Pope John Paul II calls the "greatest event in human history," namely, that God becomes man, that the Word becomes flesh, that the Son of God becomes also the Son of Mary. The Incarnation is truly the life-event that gives all the rest of life its meaning! It becomes the focal point of all human history, marking its center, dividing what went before from what would come after: B.C. versus A.D.

Let us reflect for a moment on Our Lady, chosen to be the Mother of God. What a great privilege! But we must not forget that Mary had to cooperate with God's grace in her call to divine motherhood. She had to have great faith, never doubting God's plan for her. As

Elizabeth, her elderly cousin, said at the Visitation: "And blessed is she who believed that there would be a fulfilment of what was spoken to her from the Lord" (Luke 1:45). She had to have a profound humility, ready to serve God as He wanted her to: "Behold, I am the handmaid of the Lord" (Luke 1:38). She had to have an enormous love for God to embrace His will in complete trust, for His glory and the world's salvation: "Let it be to me according to your word!" (Luke 1:38). In the beautiful words of Mother Teresa of Calcutta: "Mary gave God permission!" Only then did the Holy Spirit overshadow Our Lady. Only then did the Word become flesh within her. Only then did God's Son become also Mary's Son.

## 6

# The Holy Spirit and Our Sharing in Mary's Maternal Role

St. Augustine taught that Our Lady had conceived Jesus spiritually in her soul before she ever conceived Him physically in her body. Both "conceptions" were results of the Holy Spirit working within her. Jesus was already living in the heart of Our Lady by faith and love (before He took flesh in her womb at the Annunciation). St. Paul tells us that something similar must happen in our own lives so "that Christ may dwell in your hearts through faith"(Ephesians 3:17). How does this happen? By faithfully keeping Jesus' word (cf. John 14:23), just as Our Lady did. By doing what pleases God each day, like Mary, we "give God permission" to act in our lives. The Holy Spirit then forms Jesus spiritually within us! He transforms our minds and hearts to resemble the mind and heart of Jesus Himself more closely. Our thoughts, our words, and our deeds become so thoroughly permeated with Jesus' likeness that we can say with St. Paul, "It is no longer I who live, but Christ who lives in me" (Galatians 2:20).

This is actually a share in Our Lady's maternal role and relationship with Jesus. On one occasion, when Jesus was teaching in a crowded place, He was told that His mother and other relatives were waiting to speak with Him. Jesus said, "Who is my mother, and who are my brethren? . . . Whoever does the will of my Father in heaven is my brother, and sister, and mother" (Matthew 12:48, 50). By His words, Jesus was not taking anything away from the holiness of His mother. Rather, He was showing us precisely where it really lay, namely, in her doing the Father's will so completely. Now, when we also do our Heavenly Father's will, we share in Mary's role as mother of Jesus. How do we do this? St. Francis explains this point when he says we are "mothers of Jesus" when we carry Him spiritually in our hearts (as Mary carried Him in her womb), when we bring Him to others in their need by our works of mercy (as Mary brought Him to Elizabeth in her need), and when we help Him come to spiritual birth in others by sharing God's Word in the Gospel message and by the authentic Christian witness of our daily lives (as Mary did at Cana, moving Jesus to reveal His glory, which in turn moved His disciples to believe in Him — cf. John 2:11). St. Paul expresses this same sentiment in another place when he writes: "My little children, with whom I am again in travail until Christ be formed in you!" (Galatians 4:19). Let us resolve to imitate Our Lady and to share daily in her "motherly role" in regard to Jesus.

# 7

# "New Life in Christ Through Water and the Spirit"

Every Christian actually lives two lives at the same time. One is his "earthly life," or "natural life." This begins at the moment of his conception and continues after birth until the day of his death. The other is his "new life in Christ," which begins on the day of his Baptism. It is meant to continue for all eternity (unless impeded by unrepented mortal sin). This is his "supernatural life," or life in the Spirit.

Jesus' teaching on Baptism is found in his dialogue with a prominent Pharisee named Nicodemus (cf. John 3:1-15). He was a member of the Jewish governing assembly called the Sanhedrin. He came to speak to Jesus "under cover of night" because it was not considered "politically correct" to be seen speaking with Him. Jesus makes two important statements about Baptism, the sacrament that confers our new life in Christ. First Jesus says, "Truly, truly, I say to you, unless one is born anew he cannot see the kingdom of God" (John 3:3). This statement stresses the importance of Baptism: it is needed to enter the Kingdom of God. A key word here in Greek is *anothen*. This word has two meanings. One of them is "again" in the sense of "a second time." The other meaning is "from above." Nicodemus took the word in the sense of a second or repeated natural birth. So he ends up asking, "How can a man be born when he is old? Can he enter a second time into his mother's womb and be born?" (John 3:4). This is obviously not what Our Lord meant.

So Jesus answers Nicodemus with a second important statement: "Truly, truly, I say to you, unless one is born of water and the Spirit, he cannot enter the kingdom of God" (John 3:5). This "new birth" Jesus speaks about is to be born "from above." Jesus is using *anothen* in this sense of "from above." Since it is "from above," it is a real supernatural experience. It is to be a supernatural life. It enables us to live a life "above" the level and destiny of our natural earthly life that ends in death.

Jesus said this new life is given through water and the Holy Spirit. "Water" is a symbol for life, since all living creatures need water to survive. It is also a symbol for cleansing, since we use water for bathing and washing things. The external sign of the pouring of water in the Sacrament of Baptism, therefore, indicates both a cleansing away of sin and a coming to new life. At the same time that the water is being poured (along with the words of the baptismal formula: "I baptize you in the Name of the Father, and of the Son, and of the Holy Spirit"), the Holy Spirit comes into our soul. It is His presence now in the soul that brings about the remission of sins (Original Sin and personal sins) as well as being the source of a new life by which the soul participates in God's own nature and life. It is by sharing God's life through "sanctifying grace" in this world that we are being prepared to share His eternal life in the glory of heaven. This is obviously another reason why we call the Holy Spirit "the Giver of Life."

# 8

# Baptism as Death and Life

In our last reflection, we focused on Jesus' teaching that Baptism is a birth to a new life through water and the Holy Spirit. In this reflection, we turn to St. Paul who further enlightens us about the nature of Baptism. He tells us that it involves both death and life in Christ. St. Paul writes:

> Do you not know that all of us who have been baptized into Christ Jesus were baptized into his death? We were buried therefore with him by baptism into death, so that as Christ was raised from the dead by the glory of the Father, we too might walk in newness of life.
>
> For if we have been united with him in a death like his, we shall certainly be united with him in a resurrection like his.
>
> — Romans 6:3-5

What is St. Paul telling us here? He is first of all using the ceremony of Baptism by immersion, as opposed to the simpler form of pouring water on the forehead of the person to be baptized. In immersion, the person being baptized is totally immersed three times in a body of water such as a river or lake. Both the celebrant (a priest or deacon) and the person to be baptized usually stand in the water about waist high. In the ceremony, when the celebrant says, "I baptize you in the Name of the Father. . . ," he immerses the person fully, dunking him head and all into the water. When the person rises up from the water, he is immersed a second time when the celebrant says, ". . . and of the Son . . ."; finally, the person is immersed a third time when the celebrant says the concluding words of the baptismal formula, ". . . and of the Holy Spirit. Amen."

St. Paul tells us that this triple immersion into the water followed each time by a rising from the water indicates a process of dying and rising with Christ. The body of water represents a tomb or death. When the person, therefore, is immersed into the water, it signifies his dying with Christ, his being buried in the tomb with Jesus. What dies in us at this moment? The "old self" of sin (cf. Ephesians 4:22) — Original Sin and, in the case of those who have attained the use of reason, any actual sins (personal sins) the individual has committed. What happens to these sins? They are completely wiped away or destroyed by the redemptive power of Jesus through the working of the Holy Spirit, the Sanctifier. In fact, these sins are so completely annihilated in Baptism that any personal sins committed before Baptism are never brought to the Sacrament of Penance, which is meant for the forgiveness only of sins committed after Baptism.

Each time the person being baptized rises up from the water, it indicates his rising to new life in Jesus. It is like a personal resurrection with Jesus from the tomb of sin to share His risen life, the very beginning of eternal life!

# 9

# Our Daily Dying and Rising with Christ Is the Special Work of the Holy Spirit

We have seen that Baptism means death and life in Jesus. St. Paul explains that all the baptized share in a dying with Jesus to sin and a rising with Jesus to a new life of holiness as befits our new status as children of God. He sums up this point in a powerful statement: "The death he [Jesus] died he died to sin, once for all, but the life he lives he lives to God. So you also must consider yourselves dead to sin and alive to God in Christ Jesus" (Romans 6:10-11).

If we die immediately after our Baptism, we would go straight to heaven because the sacrament removes all sin. We would be totally purified so as to be able to enter the glorious presence of God. (We should remember that anyone with even the slightest residue of sin on his soul would not want to enter God's all-holy presence because he would feel absolutely unworthy.) We would be perfectly happy in heavenly bliss. However, our spiritual capacity would not reach its full potential or maturity. That comes as we live our spiritual life here on earth, living in the state of sanctifying grace, practicing the virtues, especially faith, hope, and love, and fulfilling God's holy will.

All of this involves us in a daily spiritual struggle. As 1 John 2:16 points out, we encounter the opposition of our three primary spiritual enemies, namely: (1) the world — "the concupiscence of the eyes," that is, the lure of earthly power and possessions; (2) the flesh — "the concupiscence of the flesh," or sexual lust; and (3) the devil — "the pride of life." In addition, we experience within us what St. Thomas Aquinas called "the wounds of Original Sin." "Ignorance" or lack of proper knowledge affects our minds; "malice" or a tendency to choose things pleasing to us rather than to God affects our wills. In addition, our passions and emotions are affected by a certain disorder. Our emotions that deal with pleasure and pain in our lives are affected by a disorder called "concupiscence," which blindly seeks carnal pleasures even contrary to God's will; our other emotions, which help us attain useful but difficult goals, are now affected by a wound called "timidity," which makes us shrink back in the face of fear and discouragement.

We are caught up in a veritable "spiritual warfare." In the words of the Book of Sirach, "My son, if you come forward to serve the Lord, / prepare yourself for temptation. . . . / For gold is tested in the fire, / and acceptable men in the furnace of humiliation" (Sirach 2:1, 5). We should see these trials as the continued living out of our Baptism. In the sacrament we died to sin. In the baptismal promises we renounced sin and Satan, the prince of darkness. In our daily struggles we keep repeating that renunciation, not only in our words but more importantly in our deeds. In Baptism we came to new life in Christ through the power of the Holy Spirit. We professed our faith in the Most Holy Trinity and in the Catholic Church and all that she teaches. Now, we must remain faithful to our profession of faith.

St. Paul expresses our experience of the daily struggle in terms reminiscent of the experience of Baptism as a dying and rising with Christ. He writes:

> [We are] always carrying in the body the death of Jesus, so that the life of Jesus may be manifested in our bodies. For while we live we are always being given up to death for Jesus' sake, so that the life of Jesus may be manifested in our mortal flesh.
>
> — 2 Corinthians 4:10-11

It is the Holy Spirit Who strengthens us to be victorious in this spiritual warfare. So let us invoke the help of the Holy Spirit that in our daily struggles we may die ever more fully to sin and live ever more fully our new life in Christ. Let us remember St. Paul's counsel to his disciple Timothy to "stir into flame" the gift of the Holy Spirit Who dwelt in him because "God did not give us a spirit of timidity but a spirit of power and love and self-control" (2 Timothy 1:7).

# PART IV

## We Believe in . . . Him Who Proceeds from the Father and the Son

## 10

# The Holy Spirit's Relationship to the Father and the Son

Our present reflection touches on one of the deepest aspects of our Catholic Faith. It pertains to the inner life of the Most Blessed Trinity. We are finite creatures; God is an infinite Creator. How can we, so limited by space and time, grasp the reality of God Who is at once both infinite and eternal? It is only with God's revelation and grace, and even then our grasp will be very limited.

An experience is related in the life of St. Augustine of Hippo, perhaps the greatest mind in the history of the Catholic Church, that helps explain the difficulty. He was reflecting on the mystery of the Blessed Trinity, trying to understand how God could be one in nature, yet three in Persons. While meditating, he was walking along the shore of the Mediterranean Sea. He suddenly became distracted by a little boy playing in the sand. The child had dug a hole in the sand, and with a little pail he was taking water from the sea and pouring it into the hole he had dug. The saint went over to the child and asked what he was doing. The child answered that he was going to put all the water in the sea into the hole. The saint told the little boy that he could not do that because the sea was too great and the hole was too small. Then the child told the saint that neither could he with his limited mind ever understand God, Who is infinite. Some say that it was the Christ Child Who spoke to the saint, others that it was an angel. In any case, the saint concluded that to understand God, a person would have to be God, and that God is really more unlike what we think Him to be than like it!

Having stated the difficulty of our task, we can still ask: What can we say of the Holy Spirit's relationship to the Father and the Son? Let us answer by using a common, simple explanation. The Three Divine Persons share a truly communal life. After all, if we human beings are made in God's image and likeness (cf. Genesis 1:26), our life must reflect even very faintly something of God's own inner divine life. We humans are related by the community called family. Sometimes we even speak of the life of the Blessed Trinity as "the Family of God." Now in the New Testament, when Jesus, the Second Divine Person Who became man, revealed His relationship to the First Divine Person, He expressed it in family or communal terms, namely, as the Son to the Father.

In the study of theology, we say that the Father is the source, or fountainhead, of the Blessed Trinity because He begets God the Son eternally. In the Nicene Creed, we say of the Son that He is "begotten, not made." If He were "made," it would imply that there was a time that He did not exist. That, in turn, would mean that the Son was not God, since God is eternal — He always was, He always is, and He always will be. So, we cannot say that the Son is "made" by the Father. However, He is "begotten" in the sense that He comes forth from the Father eternally.

How does the Father "beget" His Divine Son? In the Trinity, God has two supreme powers: His divine intellect and His divine will. In His intellect, the Father has an image of Himself that is so infinitely perfect it is the Second

Divine Person. Let us use a comparison. An artist has in his mind an image of himself. From that image, he paints a portrait of himself that is an exact likeness. However, the artist does not have the power to make that image come alive. In the Godhead, the Heavenly Father's infinitely perfect image of Himself is alive. This image is God the Son. Another way of looking at this is to realize that we express the ideas in our minds in our words. In a sense, we can say that God the Father "begets" His Divine Son by speaking His Word eternally. It is an intellectual generation, since God is spiritual and not physical. St. John, in the Prologue of his Gospel, calls the Second Divine Person "the Word": "In the beginning was the Word, and the Word was with God, and the Word was God"(John 1:1).

Besides His divine intellect, God also has His divine will. Love comes from the will. Now, God the Father and God the Son love each other with a Love that is infinitely perfect. This mutual infinitely perfect "Love" of the Father and the Son is the Third Divine Person, the Holy Spirit. This is why the Nicene Creed says of the Holy Spirit that He "proceeds from the

Father and the Son." Again, a human comparison can help. A child is conceived as a result of the loving sexual relationship of his or her parents. Similarly, the Holy Spirit is brought forth as the mutual, eternal, infinite "Love" of the Father and the Son. Theologians use the rather mysterious term "spiration" (from the Latin *spirare,* "to breathe") to explain the process by which the Holy Spirit "proceeds from the Father and the Son."

We can sum this up by saying the Son of God is "begotten" by an intellectual generation in the mind of God the Father, Who expresses His divine image or Word eternally. The Holy Spirit "proceeds," or comes forth, by an act of the mutual divine will of the Father and the Son as the eternal, infinite expression of their Love. In our next reflection, we shall look at some of the consequences of the Son of God as the "Word" and the Holy Spirit as "Love."

# 11

# The Works of Each of the Three Divine Persons

In this reflection, we will look at two principles in dogmatic theology regarding the Blessed Trinity that are very helpful here. The first principle deals with the inner life of the Blessed Trinity. As mentioned in the previous reflection, the Three Divine Persons are distinct in their relationships to one another. The Father begets the Son by an eternal generation of the mind. The Holy Spirit proceeds from the Father and the Son by an eternal mutual spiration of the will.

> *The divine persons are relative to one another.* Because it does not divide the divine unity, the real distinction of the persons from one another resides solely in the relationships that relate them to one another: "In the relational names of the persons the Father is related to the Son, the Son to the Father, and the Holy Spirit to both [the

> Father and the Son]. While they are called three persons in view of their relations [to one another], we believe [they are] one in nature or substance." Indeed "everything (in them) is one where there is no opposition of relationship."
>
> — CCC, 255

The second principle applies to the relationship of the Blessed Trinity to everything outside their own inner Trinitarian life, namely, to all creatures. In this regard, all Three Divine Persons always work together as one in the unity of their nature in relationship to everything they created. There is one exception, however, and that is that only the Second Divine Person, God the Son, became man. God the Father did not become incarnate, nor did God the Holy Spirit, but only God the Son.

> The whole divine economy [creation, redemption, sanctification] is the common work of the three divine persons. For as the Trinity has only one and the same nature, so too does it have only one and the same

operation: "The Father, the Son, and the Holy Spirit are not three principles of creation but one principle." However, each divine person performs the common work according to his unique personal property. . . . It is above all the divine missions of the Son's Incarnation and the gift of the Holy Spirit that show forth the properties of the divine persons.

— CCC, 258

The last part of this quote from the *Catechism* expresses an important point regarding all God's works on behalf of His creatures. In theology, we "attribute" or assign or designate to each of the Divine Persons a certain "work" that reflects their relationship in the Trinity and in the plan of salvation. Now, there are three great "works" in God's plan of salvation: creation, redemption, and sanctification.

The work of creation is attributed in a special way to God the Father, although, as we have said, all Three Divine Persons carried out the work of creation together. Why? Because the Father is the source, or fountainhead, of the life of the Blessed Trinity. So, He is seen fittingly as the source of all other life and all creation. All comes ultimately from Him. As we say in the Nicene Creed, "We believe in one God, the Father, the Almighty, maker of heaven and earth, of all that is seen and unseen. . . ."

The work of redemption is attributed to God the Son, although all Three Divine Persons were involved in the work of redemption. Remember, as we pointed out already, only God the Son became man. As man, He carried out the human deeds of the redemption by His life, death, and resurrection. It is for this reason that the work of redemption is especially attributed to God the Son.

The work of sanctification is attributed to the Holy Spirit. To sanctify means to make someone or something holy. Now the works of sanctification are seen as works of love. Since the Holy Spirit is the personified eternal Love of the Father and the Son, the works of sanctification are especially seen as carried out by Him. Remember, however, that the Three Divine Persons actually carry out all these works together.

In our next few reflections, we shall look at some of the individual works of sanctification especially attributed to the Holy Spirit, Who is Love.

## 12

# The Incarnation (Part 1)

The Incarnation is at the heart of the faith of the Catholic Church and the lives of all who call themselves Christian. It expresses the belief that Jesus Christ is the Son of God, the Second Divine Person of the Blessed Trinity, Who became man. He took His human nature from the Blessed Virgin Mary of Nazareth and united it to His divine nature. Pope John Paul II has said that the Incarnation is the greatest event in human history. In the words of St. Francis, through the Incarnation "the Lord of Majesty became our Brother." Jesus' very birth marks the center of human history, at least in the Western world, dividing it in half, "B.C." ("Before Christ") and "A.D." ("Anno Domini," or "In the Year of the Lord").

As we have seen in our previous reflections, the Incarnation is a work of love carried out by all Three Divine Persons. God the

Father so loved the world that He sent His Only-Begotten Son into it to win eternal life for us (cf. John 3:16). God the Son loved us so much that He came and freely laid down His life for us that we in turn might have life and have it to the full (cf. John 10:10). God the Holy Spirit loved us so much that He overshadowed Our Lady at the Annunciation that she might conceive and bear as her Son the Savior of the world (cf. Luke 1:35-38).

At the same time, however, we do acknowledge the special role of the Holy Spirit in bringing about the Incarnation. As we say in the Nicene Creed, "[Jesus] was conceived by the Holy Spirit and born of the Virgin Mary." The Spirit's role in this work of holiness stems from His being the personified Love of the Father and the Son.

Let us close our reflection with the following beautiful thoughts from the *Catechism of the Catholic Church*:

> The mission of the Holy Spirit is always conjoined and ordered to that of the Son. The Holy Spirit, "the Lord, the giver of Life," is sent to sanctify the womb of the Virgin

Mary and divinely fecundate it, causing her to conceive the eternal Son of the Father in a humanity drawn from her own.

— CCC, 485

The Father's only Son, conceived as man in the womb of the Virgin Mary, is "Christ," that is to say, anointed by the Holy Spirit from the beginning of His human existence, though the manifestation of this fact takes place only progressively: to the shepherds, to the magi, to John the Baptist, to the disciples. Thus the whole life of Jesus Christ will make manifest "how God anointed Jesus of Nazareth with the Holy Spirit and with power."

— CCC, 486

# 13

# The Incarnation (Part 2)

In this reflection, we shall look in more depth at the Holy Spirit's work of love in the Incarnation, using certain teachings in the *Catechism of the Catholic Church* as a guide. The *Catechism* sums up all the marvelous works of the Holy Spirit in the life of Our Lady in a simple yet profound statement: "In her, the 'wonders of God' that the Spirit was to fulfill in Christ and the Church began to be manifested" (CCC, 721). In other words, the absolute holiness of the humanity of Jesus, seen in His total obedience to the will of His Heavenly Father, in His charity, meekness, humility, poverty, chastity, mercy, compassion, and all the virtues, was already evident in the life of Our Lady but, of course, in a much more limited degree.

Furthermore, the holiness that was present imperfectly in the Catholic Church during her earthly pilgrimage, witnessed by the lives of holy people (traditionally called the "Church Militant") — as well as the fullness of holiness that will be present in the Church at the end of time (cf. Revelation 21:1-2) when she will be the "spotless Bride of Christ" (traditionally called the "Church Triumphant") — is already seen in the holiness of Our Lady. It was certainly with good reason that St. Maximilian Mary Kolbe, the Conventual Franciscan friar who became the "martyr of charity" at Auschwitz, called Our Lady "the Masterpiece of the Holy Spirit."

The *Catechism* next presents four specific ways in which the Holy Spirit carried out in Our Lady the great mystery of the Incarnation, the supreme work of His love.

First, He adorned Our Lady for the Incarnation by the graces of her Immaculate Conception so that she might become a beautiful dwelling place for the Eternal Word Who would take flesh within her. Not only did the Holy Spirit preserve her from any stain of Original Sin, but He also filled her with a fullness of grace, making her uniquely prepared to receive and to respond fully to Jesus' love.

> The Holy Spirit *prepared* Mary by his grace. It was fitting that the mother of him in whom "the whole fullness of deity dwells bodily" [*Col* 2:9] should herself be "full of grace." She was, by sheer grace, conceived without sin as the most humble of creatures, the most capable of welcoming the inexpressible gift of the Almighty.
>
> — CCC, 722

Second, Mary was the chosen instrument through which the Holy Spirit would carry out the Heavenly Father's plan to send His Son into the world. It would be a marvelous work of love: "Behold, a virgin shall conceive and bear a son, / and his name shall be called Emmanuel [which means 'God with us']" (Matthew 1:23).

The *Catechism* tells us:

> In Mary, the Holy Spirit *fulfills* the plan of the Father's loving goodness. [With and] through the Holy Spirit, the Virgin conceives and gives birth to the Son of God. By the Holy Spirit's power and her faith, her virginity became uniquely fruitful.
>
> — CCC, 723

Third, once Jesus had been conceived, the Holy Spirit used Our Lady as His first and most splendid cooperator in presenting Jesus to others, such as her aged cousin, St. Elizabeth, and her unborn child, St. John the Baptist, as well as to the shepherds of Bethlehem and the Wise Men from the East.

> In Mary, the Holy Spirit *manifests* the Son of the Father, now become the Son of the Virgin. She is the burning bush of the definitive theophany. Filled with the Holy Spirit she makes the Word visible in the humility of his flesh. It is to the poor and the first representatives of the gentiles that she makes him known.
>
> — CCC, 724

Fourth, following from Our Lady's role of introducing Jesus to others, the Holy Spirit uses her to help form a lasting bond of communion with Jesus, through a living and growing faith and love. This becomes the bond of discipleship.

Finally, through Mary, the Holy Spirit begins to bring men, the objects of God's merciful love, *into communion* with Christ. And the humble are always the first to accept Him: shepherds, magi, Simeon and Anna, the bride and groom at Cana, and the first disciples.

— CCC, 725

14

# The Holy Spirit and the Holy Eucharist (Part 1)

In our two previous reflections, we have seen how the Incarnation is the greatest expression of God's love for us, because by it God Himself became man. Furthermore, we recognize that although it is the work of all Three Divine Persons together, we attribute it in a special way to the Holy Spirit. This is because, as we have already seen, the Holy Spirit Himself is the eternal, personal Love of the Father and the Son for one another. In other words, in the Holy Trinity we credit the One Who is "Love" with carrying out in a special way all those works that spring from Divine Love.

The next great work of love we attribute in a special way to the Holy Spirit is His role in the change of ordinary bread and wine into the very body, blood, soul, and divinity of Jesus Christ during the Holy Sacrifice of the Mass. This change is called "Transubstantiation." It simply means that when a validly ordained Catholic priest, acting in the Person of Christ *(in persona Christi)*, says the words Jesus said at the Last Supper when He instituted the Eucharist — namely, " 'This is my body' . . . 'This is my blood' " (Matthew 26:26, Mark 14:22, cf. Luke 22:19-20) — the substances of bread and wine are changed into the body and blood of Jesus Christ. The "accidents" of bread and wine — namely, their appearance, size, shape, quantity, taste, color, texture, and the like — remain the same. As a result, the Eucharistic Bread still looks like ordinary bread, but it is now the "body of Jesus." In a similar way, the cup of wine just consecrated is no longer simply ordinary table wine, but it is now the precious blood of Jesus Christ.

This awesome change is accomplished in every Holy Sacrifice of the Mass at the moment of the Consecration. How is this change brought about? Our Catholic Faith teaches that it occurs when the priest says the same words of institution Jesus used at the Last Supper — " 'This is my body' . . . 'This is my blood' " — over the bread and wine that have been prepared upon the altar.

> The Catholic Church adheres firmly to the view that the priest [brings about] the "transubstantiation" solely by the uttering of the words of institution. The "Decree for the Armenians" teaches with St. Thomas, "The words of the Savior which he used when he made this Sacrament are the form of the Sacrament; the priest then speaking (these words) in the person of Christ effects this Sacrament." . . . The Council of Trent teaches that, according to the standing belief of the Church, "immediately after the Consecration," that is, after the uttering of the words of institution, the true Body and the true Blood of the Lord are present.
>
> — *Fundamentals of Catholic Dogma,*
> Dr. Ludwig Ott, pp. 392-393

Where, then, is the work of the Holy Spirit in the Eucharistic change of ordinary bread and wine into the very body, blood, soul, and divinity of Jesus Christ? It is seen in a prayer-invocation made to God the Father to send the Holy Spirit upon the bread and wine so that they may be made holy by becoming the very body and blood of Jesus. This prayer is called the "Epiclesis." (Actually, there is a twofold invocation of the Holy Spirit during the Eucharistic Prayer, one before and one after the Consecration of the Mass. We are speaking here of the invocation before the Consecration.) This invocation is usually accompanied by a gesture of the priest-celebrant extending his hands over the bread and wine that have been prepared for Consecration. This gesture symbolizes a calling down of the Holy Spirit on the gifts of bread and wine in order to change them. It is similar to the ceremony of the "laying on of hands" by the bishop on the heads of those being ordained, calling down the Holy Spirit upon them to fill them with the priestly power of Jesus Christ, the Eternal High Priest.

We will look more closely at the Epiclesis and the important role of the Holy Spirit in regard to the Holy Eucharist as a work of Divine Love in our next reflection. We will close this reflection, quoting the Epiclesis of Eucharistic Prayer II: "Let your Spirit come upon these gifts to make them holy, / so that they may become for us the body and blood of our Lord, Jesus Christ."

## 15

# The Holy Spirit and the Holy Eucharist (Part 2)

As we have seen in our last reflection, the Epiclesis highlights the role of the Holy Spirit in sanctifying the bread and wine by changing them into the very body and blood of Our Lord. At the same time, we must remember that all Three Divine Persons of the Blessed Trinity carry out the work of sanctification together, just as They carried out the works of creation and redemption together. This is brought out in the opening words of the Third Eucharistic Prayer: "Father, you are holy indeed, / and all creation rightly gives you praise. / All life, all holiness comes from you / through your Son, Jesus Christ our Lord, / by the working of the Holy Spirit."

Having clearly expressed here our Catholic belief that all Three Divine Persons together sanctify us, we still attribute the work of sanctification in a special way to the Holy Spirit. Why? Because sanctification of God's creatures is an act of His love for them, and the Holy Spirit is the eternal, personal Love of the Father and the Son. To repeat what was mentioned in the Preface, there is an old Latin principle in the study of theology that helps us here. It reads: *Lex credendi, lex orandi* ("The law of believing is the law of praying"). What it means is that we formulate our prayers according to what we believe. Furthermore, if we want to know what we Catholics believe, all we have to do is analyze our prayers. We will discover our Catholic truths embedded in our prayers.

Let us now look at the truly beautiful Epiclesis invocations of Eucharistic Prayers II, III, and IV, because they present the work of the Holy Spirit most clearly.

> "Let your Spirit come upon these gifts to make them holy, / so that they may become for us the body and blood of our Lord, Jesus Christ" (Prayer II).
>
> "And so, Father, we bring you these gifts. / We ask you to make them holy by the power of your Spirit, / that they may become the body and blood / of your Son,

our Lord Jesus Christ, / at whose command we celebrate this eucharist" (Prayer III).

"Father, may this Holy Spirit sanctify these offerings. / Let them become the body and blood of Jesus Christ our Lord / as we celebrate the great mystery / which he left us as an everlasting covenant" (Prayer IV).

If we analyze these three Epiclesis prayers, we find certain common elements. First, each asks God the Father to send the Holy Spirit upon the gifts, overshadowing them much as He overshadowed Our Lady at the Annunciation. Second, each invokes the Holy Spirit to "sanctify," or "make holy," the gifts of bread and wine that have been prepared. Finally, each asks that the Holy Spirit change the bread and wine into the very body and blood of Jesus. Of course, we realize that the Spirit works through the priest, who speaks in the person of Christ, reciting the words of institution.

What a great work of love takes place in every Holy Sacrifice of the Mass! In our next reflection, we shall see how the Holy Spirit, the Sanctifier, carries out a similar work of love in our own lives as He sanctifies us personally.

# 16

# Our Growth in Personal Holiness (Part 1)

In some of our previous reflections, we have already touched on the Holy Spirit's role in our personal growth in holiness. For example, we saw how we have received a new supernatural life in Christ through "water and the Spirit" (cf. Reflection 7). We also saw how that new spiritual life grows by a daily dying (to sin) and rising (to new life) in and with Christ (cf. Reflection 9) through the working of the Holy Spirit.

In this reflection, we will look once again at the Spirit's role in our personal sanctification by comparing it with His sanctifying role in the Mass. The parallel will reveal certain helpful insights. The beautiful prayer of the Epiclesis (cf. Reflection 15) will be our starting point. We have seen how this invocation, made just before the Consecration of the Mass, is a calling down of the Holy Spirit with His divine power upon the bread and wine to "sanctify" them by changing them into the body and blood of Our Lord.

Something similar happens in our lives. Let me use an example. For a moment, think of yourself as "bread" that Jesus wants to change into His own likeness. A great bishop-martyr of the first Christian century, St. Ignatius of Antioch, who died about the year 107, did just that. While on his way to Rome to be martyred by being fed to the lions, he wrote to the Christian community there and asked that they not seek a stay of his execution: "I beg you not to show me a misplaced kindness. Let me be the food of beasts that I may come to God. I am His wheat, and I shall be ground by the teeth of beasts, that I may become Christ's pure bread."

We, too, may be likened to "wheat." In place of the teeth of lions to grind us down into the flour needed to become "Christ's pure bread," life's daily trials and temptations, its disappointments and crosses of every kind, will suffice. The Holy Spirit, by His holy inspirations and sanctifying gifts, will work in us to remove sin and our attachments to it and replace them with the virtues and values of Christ

Himself. Like the bread and wine at Mass, we will be changed into the likeness of Jesus.

The late Archbishop Fulton J. Sheen, in one of his talks, said that Jesus is always in need of more "bread." In other words, He is always looking for more "bread" — meaning followers who love Him so much that they will allow themselves, like grains of wheat, to be ground down into flour in the mill of the cross so that they can become "Christ's pure bread." In this way, they are changed by the Holy Spirit. Jesus is now reliving the mysteries of His life, death, and resurrection in them, as they are spending themselves in lives of unselfish service to the Lord and to His Church. Are we ready to become "Christ's pure bread" in our own lives?

## 17

# Our Growth in Personal Holiness (Part 2)

In our last reflection, we focused on how the Holy Spirit's sanctifying mission in the Mass, seen in the changing of the bread and wine into the body and blood of Jesus, is similar to His sanctifying mission in our Christian lives, transforming us spiritually more and more into a likeness to Jesus. Now, let us compare certain significant differences in the two kinds of changes the Holy Spirit brings about.

In the Mass, for example, the bread and wine actually become the very body and blood of Jesus Christ, the Second Divine Person, Who became man. We, on the other hand, do not become Christ, but we are changed into Christ's likeness, resembling Him in mind and heart. In fact, we enter into such a spiritual union with Jesus that we can say with St. Paul, "It is no longer I who live, but Christ who lives in me"(Galatians 2:20).

At the same time, we become so "identified" with Jesus that there seems to be a bond of unity making us one with Him. For example, does Jesus not say that whatever we do to the least of His brothers and sisters we do to Him (cf. Matthew 25:40)? Furthermore, when Our Lord appeared in His glory to Saul of Tarsus along the road to Damascus to convert him, the future Apostle asked, " 'Who are you, Lord?' And he said, 'I am Jesus, whom you are persecuting' " (Acts 9:5). Notice that Our Lord did not say, "I am Jesus, whose disciples you are persecuting"!

Another significant difference in the two changes is that in the Mass, the bread and wine are totally passive as regards what is happening to them. They have absolutely no input, no say, in whether they want to be changed or not. Nor are they required to play any "cooperative part" in producing the change. All the bread and wine need to do is to be there. They are simply "acted upon" by the transforming power of the Holy Spirit.

In regard to the change in our lives, however, we must freely cooperate with the working of the Holy Spirit in us. We are persons, not things. The bread and wine, being things, have no ability to actively cooperate with the Holy Spirit's actions. In our case, God gave us a mind to know Him and a heart to love Him. God wants us to respond to His working of love in our lives as the persons He created us to be. We must use our intelligence and free will. St. Augustine (died 430) summed this up many centuries ago in a famous quote: "God made us without us, but He will not save us without us!" If we do not cooperate with the Holy Spirit's sanctifying work in us, we will not become holy. He will not force holiness upon us! He will not simply "act upon" us, as He does on the bread and wine. We must give the Holy Spirit permission by cooperating freely with His inspirations and graces.

There is a third and final important difference in the two changes the Holy Spirit produces. In the Mass, the bread and wine are changed instantly and totally into the very body and blood of Jesus. As soon as the ordained priest, acting in the person of Christ, says the words of institution Jesus used at the Last Supper, " 'This is my body' . . . 'This is the cup of My Blood' " (cf. Luke 22:19-20), the bread and wine are instantly and completely changed; they are now the body and blood of Jesus Christ. In our lives, our transformation into the likeness of Jesus occurs gradually. We are changed little by little into the likeness of Jesus. As we put sin, sinful attachments, and disordered self-love out of our lives, we can be filled more and more with the new risen life we have in Christ. St. John the Baptist summed this whole process up so simply when he said, "Jesus must increase; I must decrease" (John 3:30). (Or, as another translation puts it, "Of Jesus there must be more and more; of me there must be less and less.") This is not the work of one action or of one moment (except if a person is martyred, for then the person would be cleansed completely by the shedding of his or her own blood for Jesus). It is the work of the lifetime God gives to each of us here on earth!

## 18

# The Spirit's Role in the Church's Universal Mission of Holiness

The Holy Spirit's work of sanctification is not limited only to individuals, but it extends even to the worldwide mission of the Church. After all, we exist not only as individual persons but as part of the community of God's people. The Old Covenant at Mount Sinai formed a group of Jewish exiles from Egypt into the Chosen People of God, through whom the Eternal Father prepared the world to receive His Divine Son as Lord and Savior. The New Covenant was initiated by the redemptive mission of Jesus, culminating in His saving death on the cross to take away our sins and His glorious resurrection to conquer the power of death itself. This New Covenant was inaugurated on Pentecost Sunday, when God the Father sent upon His newly Chosen People the gift of the Holy Spirit Whom Jesus had won for us as the "first fruits" of our redemption (cf. Romans 8:23).

From the first moment of that great outpouring of the Holy Spirit, His mission of guiding the Church was evident. He moved the Apostles — previously so fearful of persecution and possible suffering for the cause of Christ — to rise and speak boldly the message of Jesus' saving death and glorious resurrection. He worked many "wonders and signs" (Acts 2:43; cf. Acts 5:12) through the Apostles and others to move people to believe. This mission of the Holy Spirit has continued to our day and will continue until the end of time. He is building up the Mystical Body of Christ until it reaches its fullness, at which moment Jesus will return in glory.

Pope John Paul II has expressed his concern that Catholics come to realize the importance of the work of the Holy Spirit in the Church. He wanted this to be one of the fruits of the spiritual preparation for the Jubilee Year 2000. In paragraph 45 of his Apostolic Letter *Tertio Millennio Adveniente* ("On the Coming of the Third Millennium"), he writes:

> The primary tasks of the preparation for the Jubilee thus include *a renewed appreciation*

> *of the presence and activity of the Spirit,* who acts within the Church both in the Sacraments, especially in *Confirmation,* and in the variety of charisms, roles and ministries which he inspires for the good of the Church: "There is only one Spirit who, according to his own richness and the needs of the ministries, distributes his different gifts for the welfare of the Church (cf. *1 Cor* 12:1-11). Among these gifts stands out the grace given to the Apostles. To their authority, the Spirit himself subjected even those who were endowed with charisms (cf. *1 Cor* 14). Giving the body unity through himself and through his power and through the internal cohesion of its members, this same Spirit produces and urges love among the believers."

The Pope's words emphasize the importance of a deeper "appreciation" of the role of the Holy Spirit in the Church. This includes a heightened awareness of Who the Holy Spirit is, a greater understanding of His gifts that He uses in our personal lives (His "sanctifying gifts") and in the work of the Church (His "charismatic gifts"), and a practical response to that role on our part. In this way, we can cooperate more consciously with the Holy Spirit, not only for our own personal sanctification, but also for the growth in holiness of all our brothers and sisters in Christ. The end result will be seen in the unity and love that must characterize God's new people here on earth. Pope John Paul II calls this "*the civilization of love,* founded on the universal values of peace, solidarity, justice and liberty, which find their full attainment in Christ" (*Tertio Millennio Adveniente,* 52).

## 19

# The Spirit and the Church's Priestly Mission

Jesus' redemptive mission consisted of three aspects corresponding to His threefold Messianic role as Priest, Prophet, and King. As Priest, Jesus in His humanity sanctifies us as our Mediator with the Blessed Trinity in worship and prayer. As Prophet, He taught us the eternally revealed truths we need to believe and live by in order to gain everlasting life. As King, He came, not to be served, but to spend Himself in humble service of His brothers and sisters, ultimately laying down His life on the cross out of love for them. Now, the Holy Spirit has come to complete Jesus' redemptive mission: "And that we might live no longer for ourselves but for him [Jesus], / he sent the Holy Spirit from you, Father, / as his first gift to those who believe, / to complete his work on earth / and bring us the fullness of grace" (Eucharistic Prayer IV).

All members of the Church carry on this threefold mission of Jesus, with the Holy

Spirit working in, with, and through them all. Let us look first at the Church's priestly mission of worship and prayer. All Catholics share in the priesthood of Jesus Christ. The laity do so by Baptism and Confirmation; the clergy also do so by Holy Orders. By the power of the Holy Spirit Whom they received in ordination, the clergy can offer the Holy Sacrifice of the Mass. The laity, through a share in the priestly power of Jesus in the priesthood of the faithful (cf. 1 Peter 2:5) received through the Sacrament of Baptism, participate in the manner of the laity in the Holy Sacrifice of the Mass.

The merits of the Mass do not benefit only the priest or just the other people who are present and participate. They extend outwardly and affect the salvation and sanctification of the whole world. This comes principally by renewing, in an unbloody manner, the sacrifice Jesus offered of Himself on the cross on Good Friday for our sakes. In addition, many of the prayers at Mass reach out to the needs of the whole Church, indeed the whole world. The Prayer of the Faithful usually includes both general and specific intentions of need — for example, for Church and world leaders, respect for life, peace and justice concerns, natural and man-made tragedies, special occasions (such as marriages and ordinations), the sick, the dying, and the faithful departed. Within the Eucharistic Prayer itself, there is always a remembrance of the Pope and the local bishop, as well as the faithful wherever they may be as well as those in purgatory.

The Mass, indeed, has a powerful social effect on the whole Mystical Body. So, too, do the sacraments. Though they are received by individuals, they have a ripple effect that spreads out to others. St. Paul teaches that when one member of the Mystical Body suffers, all the other members suffer with it; but when one member is doing well, all the other members around it benefit (cf. 1 Corinthians 12:26). So when a person receives Baptism, for example, the grace of the sacrament is given only to that individual alone. He or she becomes a child of God. However, he or she also becomes joined to the whole Mystical Body of Christ, with gifts and responsibilities and a God-given mission that will ultimately benefit all members of Christ.

Again, in Confirmation only the individual is confirmed; however, he or she now has a quasi-official office to promote the Faith to others and to defend it when it is under attack. That is a social benefit to the whole Church, which the Holy Spirit uses to promote the Church's mission of evangelization.

Marriage, too, is a sacrament that extends beyond its "unitive purpose" of the mutual love of husband and wife. It extends by its "procreative purpose," at least in potential, to begetting new life for the human family and ultimately for the kingdom of heaven. Even Holy Orders is not directed primarily to the benefit of the individual man being ordained but to the good of the whole Church by providing ordained ministers to carry out the sacred actions of Christ.

Moreover, Confession, personalized as that sacrament is because it involves the forgiveness of the sins of an individual, also has a powerful social effect. Not only will it allow the conversion from a life of imprisonment to sin to a life of the freedom of the children of God, but the good example that will follow from that conversion will have a powerful effect on those who come to know of it. One only needs to reflect on how many sinners found confidence and encouragement for their own conversions by reading the conversion story of St. Augustine in his *Confessions*. The same is true of the Sacrament of the Holy Eucharist. In the same way that a chain is strengthened as each link becomes stronger, so the Body of Christ, the Church, is strengthened as each of her children is fed with the Bread of Life. The Church's children will have life in Christ more abundantly.

Finally, even the Sacrament of the Sick has powerful positive effects for the sanctification of the universal Church. If God gives healing through the sacramental anointing and the invocation of the Holy Spirit upon the sick person, the faith of many is strengthened. The sick person can generally be restored to a useful place in the family (barring extreme old age). On the other hand, if there is no bodily healing, there can certainly be a spiritual strengthening to accept the cross of suffering and bear it more patiently with Jesus for the good of His Mystical Body, the Church.

In all the sacraments, then, the Holy Spirit is at work, not only sanctifying the individuals directly involved, but spreading holiness throughout the Church, even pervading the whole world, like yeast in a mound of dough.

## 20

# The Spirit and the Church's Prophetic Mission

In this reflection we will focus on the Catholic Church's prophetic or teaching mission and how the Holy Spirit guides it for the salvation and sanctification of the whole world. The Sacred Scriptures make it very clear that the Holy Spirit guides the Church in her mission of worldwide evangelization. Just before He ascended into heaven, Jesus gave His Apostles the mission to go forth and teach all nations everything He had taught them. In this way, they would make disciples of all the nations and baptize all who would believe in the name of the Blessed Trinity, the Father, the Son, and the Holy Spirit (cf. Matthew 28:18-20).

The Holy Spirit's work of guiding evangelization throughout the Church can be seen in His role as the Paraclete, the Spirit of Truth. Jesus stresses this role in the Last Supper account of St. John's Gospel. There He tells us that the Spirit of Truth will be with the Church always (cf. John 14:16-17). The Holy Spirit will furthermore instruct us in everything and remind us constantly of all that Jesus Himself has taught us (cf. John 14:26). In addition, the Paraclete will bear witness to Jesus by working signs and wonders to confirm the truth of those Christians who give witness to Jesus either by living exemplary lives or by preaching and teaching about Jesus (cf. John 15:26-27). The Spirit of Truth will ultimately guide us to all truth. Finally, He will "prove the world wrong" for its lack of faith in Jesus, demonstrating by the signs and wonders done in Jesus' name that the Father has glorified Him in heaven. He will, at the same time, show that it is the devil, "the prince of this world," who has suffered the real defeat and eternal condemnation (cf. John 16:8-11).

In carrying out His mission of evangelization, the Spirit of Truth works through the whole Mystical Body, clergy and laity alike. Speaking of the "new evangelization" to which every person from the Pope down to the newest baptized member of the Church is being called at this time, Pope John Paul II, in his *Tertio Millennio Adveniente*, calls the Holy Spirit "the principal agent" or "the active agent" behind this great work. Like a conductor of a magnificent orchestra, the Paraclete directs all of us to fulfill our own part. St. Paul reminds us that the Mystical Body of Christ is made up of many members (cf. 1 Corinthians 12:12-31). The Holy Spirit coordinates the part of each to produce a great symphony of truth by which Jesus is honored and glorified even here on earth.

Pope John Paul II stresses the shared but different responsibility of all Catholics in proclaiming and teaching the truths of the Faith. What he says of catechetics applies to all aspects of the Church's prophetic or teaching mission:

> Catechesis always has been and always will be a work for which the whole Church must feel responsible and must wish to be responsible. But the Church's members have different responsibilities, derived from each one's mission. Because of their charge, pastors (the pope, bishops and priests) have, at differing levels, the chief responsibility

for fostering, guiding and coordinating catechesis. For his part, the pope has a lively awareness of the primary responsibility that rests on him in this field. In this he finds reasons for pastoral concern but principally a source of joy and hope. Priests and religious have in catechesis a pre-eminent field for their apostolate. On another level, parents have a unique responsibility. Teachers, the various ministers of the Church, catechists, and also organizers of social communications, all have in various degrees very precise responsibilities in this education of the believing conscience, an education that is important for the life of the Church and affects the life of society as such.

— Apostolic Exhortation
*Catechesi Tradendae*
("Catechesis in Our Time"), 16

For the Church to function effectively, each member must carry out his or her part. Each part is important. If a person fails to carry out his or her assigned task in the "new evangelization," or does it poorly or, worse still, distorts the truth meant to be conveyed, the

Spirit's work and the Church's mission are hindered. In such a case, we could apply the old saying "If you are not part of the solution, then you are part of the problem." Let us pray, then, that the Spirit of Truth will come and lead us into all truth (cf. John 16:13) and strengthen us to proclaim the truth of Jesus boldly in today's world that so desperately needs to hear the Gospel message of truth, hope, and life!

## 21

# The Spirit and the Church's Kingly Mission

When most people think of a "kingly mission," they would naturally think of royal splendor, riches, and power that surround earthly kings, queens, and other royalty. But the Christian's "kingly mission" involves just the opposite reality. It is really a mission of service. To paraphrase an old saying: "To reign [with Christ] is to serve [with Christ]."

The prophet Isaiah had already foretold Jesus would be the "Suffering Servant" of Yahweh. The prophet wrote that the Servant of Yahweh would possess the Spirit of the Lord, and that He would go about doing good, with great gentleness and compassion, establishing justice and peace among God's people:

> Behold my servant, whom I uphold, / my chosen, in whom my soul delights; / I have put my Spirit upon him, / he will bring forth justice to the nations. / He will not

> cry or lift up his voice, / or make it heard in the street; / a bruised reed he will not break, / and a dimly burning wick he will not quench; / he will faithfully bring forth justice. / He will not fail or be discouraged / till he has established justice in the earth; / and the coastlands wait for his law.
>
> — Isaiah 42:1-4

Isaiah also predicted quite graphically in one of his descriptions of the "Suffering Servant" all that He would have to suffer in order to establish ultimate peace and justice for all mankind:

> He had no form or comeliness that we should look at him, / and no beauty that we should desire him. / He was despised and rejected by men; / a man of sorrows, and acquainted with grief; . . . / Surely he has borne our griefs / and carried our sorrows; . . . / he was wounded for our transgressions, / he was bruised for our iniquities; / upon him was the chastisement that made us whole, / and with his stripes we are healed. / All we like sheep have gone astray; / we have turned

> every one to his own way; / and the Lord has laid on him / the iniquity of us all.
>
> — Isaiah 53:2-6

The mission of the "Suffering Servant" will not end in suffering, shame, and death but rather in triumph. He will be exalted in glory and bring salvation to His people:

> Yet it was the will of the Lord to bruise him; / he has put him to grief; / when he makes himself an offering for sin, / he shall see his offspring, he shall prolong his days; / the will of the Lord shall prosper in his hand; / he shall see the fruit of the travail of his soul and be satisfied; / by his knowledge shall the righteous one, my servant, / make many to be accounted righteous; / and he shall bear their iniquities. / Therefore I will divide him a portion with the great, / and he shall divide the spoil with the strong; / because he poured out his soul to death, / and was numbered with the transgressors; / yet he bore the sin of many, / and made intercession for the transgressors.
>
> — Isaiah 53:10-12

Jesus clearly identifies Himself as the "Suffering Servant" foretold by Isaiah. At His Baptism in the Jordan River by St. John the Baptist, Jesus was "anointed" for His mission as the Messiah by the Holy Spirit, Who descended upon Him in the form of a dove (cf. Luke 3:22). Now filled with the Holy Spirit, Jesus is driven by the Spirit (cf. Luke 4:1) into the desert to pray and fast for forty days, and to be tempted by the devil. When the temptations of the devil had been successfully overcome, "Jesus returned in the power of the Spirit into Galilee, and a report concerning him went out through all the surrounding country" (Luke 4:14). Jesus' "hidden life" is now over; His "public life" is about to begin. So He goes to the synagogue in Nazareth where He reads from the scroll of the prophet Isaiah part of one of the "Suffering Servant" passages:

> And he came to Nazareth, where he had been brought up; and he went to the synagogue, as his custom was, on the sabbath day. And he stood up to read; and there was given to him the book of the prophet Isaiah.

He opened the book and found the place where it was written, / "The Spirit of the Lord is upon me, / because he has anointed me to preach good news to the poor. / He has sent me to proclaim release to the captives / and recovering of sight to the blind, / to set at liberty those who are oppressed, / to proclaim the acceptable year of the Lord." / And he closed the book, and gave it back to the attendant, and sat down; and the eyes of all in the synagogue were fixed on him. And he began to say to them, "Today this scripture has been fulfilled in your hearing."

— Luke 4:16-21

In this passage from the prophet Isaiah, we find the outline of Jesus' "kingly" or "servant" mission. He will spend Himself for others, as the will of His Heavenly Father directs Him. Ultimately, that service leads to the cross, and then beyond to the resurrection. Jesus teaches us to love one another as a sign of our love for Him: "This I command you, to love one another" (John 15:17). By our Baptism, we share in Jesus' "kingly mission" of service. In the following reflections, we shall see how we can carry out this mission of service in our daily lives: doing the Father's will, imitating Jesus, being led by the Spirit of the Lord.

# 22

# The Holy Spirit and the Church's Kingly Mission as Seen in the Works of Mercy

Our mission of service can be seen clearly as we carry out what are called "the works of mercy." By these deeds, we show compassion and offer assistance to our brothers and sisters in need. Since their needs may be either of the body (corporal or physical needs) or of the soul (spiritual needs), we speak of both the "corporal" and "spiritual" works of mercy. The Catholic Church has traditionally included seven works of mercy in each category.

> *The works of mercy* are charitable actions by which we come to the aid of our neighbor in his spiritual and bodily necessities. Instructing, advising, consoling, comforting are spiritual works of mercy, as are forgiving and bearing wrongs patiently. The corporal works of mercy consist especially in feeding the hungry, sheltering the homeless,

> clothing the naked, visiting the sick and imprisoned, and burying the dead. Among all these, giving alms to the poor is one of the chief witnesses to fraternal charity: it is also a work of justice pleasing to God.
>
> — CCC, 2447

In carrying out the corporal and spiritual works of mercy, we accomplish three important aspects of our Christian vocation. First, we imitate Jesus Who said He had come to serve and not to be served. In the Gospel accounts we read of Jesus having pity on the crowds who were like sheep without a shepherd. As a result, despite His own need for food and rest and that of the Apostles with Him, He preached at great length to the people who hungered to be instructed by the Word of God (cf. Mark 6:34). Jesus was carrying out the spiritual work of mercy: "to instruct the ignorant [uninformed]." On other occasions, Jesus multiplied bread "to feed the hungry," as when He would not dismiss a large crowd of people who had been with Him for days because they had no food, and He was concerned that while they were returning to their homes, they might faint along the wayside from their lack of nourishment (cf. Matthew 15:32 and Mark 8:2-3).

Second, in our practice of the works of mercy, we can serve Jesus Himself! I had this brought home to me very vividly in conversation with Mother Teresa of Calcutta. She spontaneously said to me one day, "How much we need the poor and needy! We will only know in heaven how many graces came to us through our opportunity to serve them in their need." Then she added a very powerful statement, "We cannot do anything for God in heaven! In heaven He has everything He needs. So, God became man. Now we can do something for Him, because He said, 'I was hungry, and you fed me. I was thirsty, and you gave me something to drink.' " What a powerful insight by a saintly woman whose life was marked by a generous service of the poor. Her insight may well have come from her meditation on a passage of Sacred Scripture she often quoted in her talks, namely, Jesus' description of the Last Judgment, where we find mention of all but one ("to bury the dead") of the "corporal works of mercy":

> Then the King will say to those at his right hand, "Come, O blessed of my Father, inherit the kingdom prepared for you from the foundation of the world; for I was hungry and you gave me food, I was thirsty and you gave me drink, I was a stranger and you welcomed me, I was naked and you clothed me, I was sick and you visited me, I was in prison and you came to me." Then the righteous will answer him, "Lord, when did we see thee hungry and feed thee, or thirsty and give thee drink? And when did we see thee a stranger and welcome thee, or naked and clothe thee? And when did we see thee sick or in prison and visit thee?" And the King will answer them, "Truly, I say to you, as you did it to one of the least of these my brethren, you did it to me."
>
> — Matthew 25:34-40

Third, in our practice of the "works of mercy," we continue and extend the very mission of Jesus over space and time. Since we are imitating Jesus in His works of mercy, the Holy Spirit will form in us a likeness to Jesus in "mind and heart," namely, a Christlike attitude in our thoughts and a Christlike compassion in our desires. What a powerful effect this has on people! Mother Teresa of Calcutta, for example, has her Missionaries of Charity take a fourth vow — beyond poverty, chastity, and obedience — to "give free and wholehearted service to the poorest of the poor." We can only imagine the impact such an attitude of humble service must have, especially when we consider the many traditionally non-Christian countries in the world where they serve the poorest of the poor. What a great witness to Christ! Did Jesus not say, "By this all men will know that you are my disciples, if you have love for one another" (John 13:35)?

Understood correctly, the "works of mercy" are not simply a duty, they are a privilege, since we can serve Christ in one another. As Mother Teresa would often say, we can "touch Jesus" in His distressing disguise in the poor and needy. Not only do the works of mercy sanctify those who perform them, but they benefit those who are their recipients and they edify those who witness them being carried out. They are an essential part of the Holy Spirit's mission to sanctify the whole world.

## 23

# The Holy Spirit's Mission of Sanctifying the World as Seen Through the "Charismatic Gifts" He Bestows

In His conversation with the Samaritan woman at the well, Jesus referred to the Holy Spirit as the "gift of God" (John 4:10). He is truly the supreme "Gift" bestowed on us by our Heavenly Father, won for us by Jesus through His saving death and resurrection. But the Holy Spirit is not only the supreme "Gift," He is also the Divine "Gift-Giver."

Theologians distinguish two kinds of gifts given by the Holy Spirit. The first kind consists of His seven "sanctifying gifts," mentioned by the prophet Isaiah (cf. Isaiah 11:2-3), namely, wisdom, knowledge, understanding, counsel, fortitude, piety, and fear of the Lord. These gifts, which we receive along with sanctifying grace at the moment of our Baptism, are meant to make us personally holy. (The traditional Latin title for these gifts is *gratia gratum faciens*, "the gift that makes us pleasing [to God].") These gifts help us receive the daily inspirations of the Holy Spirit and put them into practice. The first four assist our minds to grasp more clearly the deep truths of our Catholic Faith and the realities of Christian life. The latter three strengthen our wills to remain firm in the face of trials, discouragement, and the demand of the daily practice of virtue and resistance to temptations.

Though the "sanctifying gifts" are actually more important for our personal growth in holiness, our focus in this reflection will be on the Holy Spirit's other kind of gifts called the "charismatic gifts." These gifts are directed at meeting various special needs within the Church community and in the exercise of her mission, so that the Mystical Body of Christ may be brought to its fullness. An important aspect of these "charismatic gifts" is that they are not given to everyone. Rather, the Holy Spirit gives them as He chooses, to whom He chooses, and for whatever purpose He chooses. (This is brought out in the traditional Latin title for these gifts: *gratiae gratis datae*, "the gifts given freely [gratis]"). St Paul writes frequently about these gifts and their importance for the Church:

> Now concerning spiritual gifts, brethren, I do not want you to be uninformed. . . . Now there are varieties of gifts, but the same Spirit; . . . To each is given the manifestation of the Spirit for the common good. . . . All these are inspired by one and the same Spirit, who apportions to each one individually as he wills.
>
> — 1 Corinthians 12:1, 4, 7, 11

St. Paul gives various lists of "charismatic gifts" (cf. 1 Corinthians 12:8-10, Romans 12:6-8, and Ephesians 4:11-12). It is generally agreed that these lists are not meant to be exhaustive listings of all charismatic gifts. In fact, it has been estimated that there are well over a hundred different charismatic gifts the Holy Spirit can confer on a person. Take, for example, the case of Padre Pio. He possessed many extraordinary gifts and phenomena, some of which St Paul does not list. They included the gifts of (1) working miracles, (2) the power of healing, (3) prophecy, (4) discernment of spirits, (5) reading hearts, (6) fragrance (the odor of sanctity), (7) bilocation, and (8) the visible stigmata. Anyone familiar with the life of Padre Pio knows what a great impact he made on countless people all around the world!

All of the charismatic gifts are important for the work of the Church, otherwise the Holy Spirit would not give them. However, some have a more powerful impact in regard to the Church's mission of universal salvation than others. Let us look at some of the gifts mentioned by St. Paul:

> To one is given through the Spirit the utterance of wisdom, and to another the utterance of knowledge according to the same Spirit, to another faith by the same Spirit, to another gifts of healing by the one Spirit, to another the working of miracles, to another prophecy, to another the ability to distinguish between spirits, to another various kinds of tongues, to another the interpretation of tongues.
>
> — 1 Corinthians 12:8-10

We can only cite as examples a few of the charismatic gifts St. Paul lists here. "Utterance of wisdom" is the gift to be able to grasp the deepest Christian truths clearly, while "the utterance of knowledge" is a gift that gives the facility to teach deep elements of the Faith in a way that they can be easily grasped by others. (I believe Archbishop Fulton J. Sheen had these gifts. In his talks and writings, he presents such penetrating insights into the teachings of the Church, and he presents them in such a way that his listeners or readers can easily follow.)

The "gifts of healing" touch many people, not only the sick who recover, but family members, friends, and others who hear of the healing received. The Spirit uses this gift to move people to a sense of gratitude toward God for the healing received. In the same way, "the working of miracles," which involves an instantaneous manifestation of God's power above and beyond the laws of Nature, often moves people to a belief in God that they might never have come to without such a powerful manifestation. (The many healings and miracles of St. Anthony of Padua made him one of the most effective preachers in all of Church history.)

"Prophecy" is the gift of acting as a spokesman for God. It could involve speaking a seemingly inspired or "anointed" message to the People of God, or foretelling things of the future, or telling a person things about his life that were hidden or even unknown to the person himself. (When Padre Pio told things to people about their lives that either they did not know at the time or did not believe could ever happen in the future, they were no doubt startled into a deeper trust in God when his words were verified.)

Finally, "the ability to distinguish between spirits" (or "discernment of spirits") is the gift that helps the faithful to know whether some phenomenon is coming from God, or from the devil, or simply from the human spirit. It is a great help in guiding people to carry out God's authentic will and to avoid the deceits of the evil one or even self-delusion.

The charismatic gifts themselves do not make the persons who possess them holy (cf. Matthew 7:21-23). However, we should pray to use faithfully any gifts the Holy Spirit may give us personally. We should also pray that the Divine Gift-Giver will pour out His gifts abundantly upon the faithful, especially in the difficult secular atmosphere we live in today. We can hope that modern "wonders and signs" (Acts 2:43) may stir up the virtue of faith in people today as they once made the Catholic Faith flourish in the pagan environment of the ancient Roman Empire.

# PART V

## We Believe . . . [That Together] with the Father and the Son He Is Worshiped and Glorified

## 24

# Equal in Divinity, Therefore Equal in the Adoration and Glory to Be Received

We begin now on another statement of the Nicene Creed, namely, that "together with the Father and the Son [the Holy Spirit] is adored and glorified." We have seen in earlier reflections how the Divinity of the Holy Spirit had been denied by some persons in Church history, especially the Macedonian heretics. The Council of Constantinople (381) condemned that heresy by defining clearly that the Holy Spirit is a Divine Person, together with the Father and the Son. The council Fathers based themselves on the baptismal formula given by Jesus, where the Father, the Son, and the Holy Spirit are mentioned on an equal level:

> All authority in heaven and on earth has been given to me. Go therefore and make disciples of all nations, baptizing them in

> the name of the Father and of the Son and of the Holy Spirit.
>
> — Matthew 28:18-19

They also recognized that the Holy Spirit had to be a Divine Person, since He sanctifies us by making us "God-like." They understood clearly that only God can make one of His creatures God-like.

The present statement of the Nicene Creed follows from the fact of the Holy Spirit's Divinity. If He is equal to the Father and the Son in Divinity, then He must be "adored and glorified" by all His creatures as They are. We give to God a unique worship and adoration we call *latria*. This supreme worship can only be given to God, because it recognizes His absolute and total dominion over our lives. After all, God made us; He sustains our existence; and we return to Him as our Judge and, if we are judged worthy, we will be with Him as our supreme happiness when our life in this world is ended. As mentioned, *latria* can only be given to God Himself, not to any angel, or saint, or even the Blessed Mother. Catholics, contrary to what some people think and other people say about us, do not worship Our Lady, or the saints, or angels. We give to the angels and saints, because of their special closeness to God, an honor called *dulia*; it is really a recognition of God's holiness in His saints and angels. To the Blessed Mother, because of her special place in the plan of God for the world's salvation as the Mother of Jesus, and because her holiness exceeds that of all the angels and saints, we give a special honor called *hyperdulia*. But never is it worship or adoration! That belongs to God alone!

How do we express our adoration of the Holy Spirit? Most obviously, we do this by praying to Him as God. This expresses our belief in His Divinity, and how much we are dependent upon Him, and how much we love Him. Our prayer may be formal or informal. Formal prayer can include, first of all, "liturgical prayer." Certainly, the celebration of the Solemnity of Pentecost focuses our prayer on the Holy Spirit, for we await Him again as the Apostles and other first disciples of Jesus did, spiritually in prayer in company with Our Lady (cf. Acts 1:14). Another liturgical celebration that focuses on the Holy Spirit is a Confirmation Mass. Such a Mass is an ideal opportunity to renew our love for the Holy Spirit, Whom we received in our own Confirmation. We can ask Him to stir up His grace in our hearts that we might better live out the meaning of our Confirmation as mature Christians and faithful witnesses for Jesus. At still other times, we can offer a votive Mass in honor of the Holy Spirit. This often happens in situations such as a "Charismatic Movement Conference" or "the Mass of the Holy Spirit" at the beginning of the academic year.

Of particular note are two hymns found in the Liturgy in honor of the Holy Spirit that make wonderful prayers (they are found in the Appendix of this book). The first is *Veni, Sancte Spiritus* ("Come, Holy Spirit"), which is the Sequence of the Mass of Pentecost Sunday. The other is the truly inspired hymn *Veni, Creator Spiritus* ("Come, Creator Spirit"), which the Church traditionally uses at the moment in ordination Masses when the Holy Spirit is being conferred by the bishop in the ceremony of the laying on of hands. When St. Teresa of Ávila began to experience mystical phenomena, including visions, she was advised to pray this prayer daily for discernment to know if these things were from God or not. After a month of praying it, the Franciscan St. Peter of Alcántara came to Ávila and confirmed for St. Teresa that her visions were from God.

Other expressions of formal prayer include the use of novenas (remember, the first novena in the Church was in preparation for Pentecost), litanies, chaplets, hymns, and devout prayers, either approved by proper Church authorities for public use or to be used privately. These can be found in various prayer books, both traditional and contemporary.

Informal prayer means the prayer that proceeds from meditation and from the stirring of the heart. It is the spontaneous outpouring of faith and love toward the Third Divine Person. Obviously, as we get to know Him more intimately on a personal basis, this will become a more significant part of our interior prayer.

As our prayer life grows, we should ask the Holy Spirit to fill us with a greater awareness of His presence and of our need to respond to Him by using the graces and inspirations He gives us daily for the honor and glory of the Most Holy Trinity as well as for our salvation and sanctification. In this way, we will be adoring and glorifying the Holy Spirit together with the Father and the Son.

# PART VI

## We Believe . . . He Has Spoken Through the Prophets

# 25

# The Holy Spirit Is Heard in the Words of the Prophets

This is the final statement of the Nicene Creed on the Holy Spirit. It reminds us that He was already at work in Old Testament times, even though His identity was only clearly revealed in the New Testament. Likewise, His mission lay hidden until Jesus, the Eternal Word Incarnate, revealed it along with His own mission during His public ministry.

The Catholic *Catechism* tells us that there were two prophetic lines developed in the Old Testament (cf. CCC, 711). The more prominent one dealt with the promise and expectation of the Messiah. This was fulfilled when "the Word became flesh" (John 1:14) at the Annunciation in Nazareth and was born in Bethlehem. The other prophetic line, less prominent, dealt with a "new Spirit" that would be poured out upon God's people. The characteristics of the awaited Messiah begin to appear in the first two verses of Isaiah 11:

> There shall come forth a shoot from the stump of Jesse, / and a branch shall grow out of his roots. / And the Spirit of the LORD shall rest upon him, / the spirit of wisdom and understanding, / the spirit of counsel and might, / the spirit of knowledge and the fear of the LORD.
>
> The Messiah's characteristics are revealed above all in the "Servant songs." These songs proclaim the meaning of Jesus' Passion and show how he will pour out the Holy Spirit to give life to the many: not as an outsider, but by embracing our "form as slave." Taking our death upon himself, he can communicate to us his own Spirit of life.
>
> —CCC, 712-713

There are many references in the Old Testament to God's desire to give to His people a "new spirit." Let us look at examples from the prophets Ezekiel and Joel:

> I will sprinkle clean water upon you, and you shall be clean from all your uncleannesses, and from all your idols will I cleanse you. A new heart I will give you,

and a new spirit I will put within you; and I will take out of your flesh the heart of stone and give you a heart of flesh. And I will put my spirit within you, and cause you to walk in my statutes and be careful to observe my ordinances.

— Ezekiel 36:25-27; cf. also
Ezekiel 11:19-20, 37:1-14

And it shall come to pass afterward, / that I will pour out my spirit on all flesh; / your sons and daughters shall prophesy, / your old men shall dream dreams, / and your young men shall see visions. / Even upon the menservants and maidservants / in those days, I will pour out my spirit.

— Joel 2:28-29

In Old Testament times, when people spoke of the "spirit of God," they did not mean the Third Divine Person of the Blessed Trinity (since His existence was only clearly revealed in the New Testament). They would have understood God's spirit to mean His power — His power to create, to give life, to direct, to console, to strengthen, and to inspire. However, it did prefigure the Holy Spirit, so that when we now look back from our New Testament vantage point, we see the Third Divine Person present and active when there is reference to God's "spirit."

He is seen acting in the lives of holy men and women who prepared the way for Jesus. The "speaking through the prophets" (cf. Nicene Creed) refers in a special way to the Word of God communicated in written form in the Sacred Scriptures.

> When the Church reads the Old Testament, she searches there for what the Spirit, "who has spoken through the prophets," wants to tell us about Christ.
>
> By "prophets" the faith of the Church here understands all whom the Holy Spirit inspired in living proclamation and in the composition of the sacred books, both of the Old and the New Testaments.
>
> — CCC, 702

In the composition of the writings of Sacred Scripture, since it was the Holy Spirit Who moved the various sacred writers to write, we consider these sacred writings to be "the Word of God." We speak of these writings as being "inspired," which means they are "breathed into" by the Holy Spirit. They have a dignity, a holiness, and a power beyond mere human words. They have the power to come alive spiritually within the person who receives them with an open heart filled with believing faith, longing hope, and generous love. They are the Word of God expressed in the language of men.

Above all, the Holy Spirit is seen as present and active in Our Lady, who marks the completion of the Old Testament time of preparation and the beginning of the New Testament fulfillment. Let us pray to Our Lady, who "kept all these things, pondering them in her heart" (Luke 2:19, cf. Luke 2:51), to give us a deep love of God's Word in the Sacred Scriptures and in her Divine Son, Jesus Christ, the Eternal Word Who became flesh in her and then dwelt among us (cf. John 1:14).

# 26

# The Holy Spirit Still Speaks Today Through Prophetic Men and Women in the Church

We have already touched on many aspects of the Holy Spirit's presence and working in the prophetic role of the Church. The Catholic *Catechism* offers a good summary of these various instances.

> The Church, a communion living in the faith of the apostles which she transmits, is the place where we know the Holy Spirit:
> — in the Scriptures he inspired;
> — in the Tradition, to which the Church Fathers are always timely witnesses;
> — in the Church's Magisterium, which he assists;
> — in the sacramental liturgy, through its words and symbols, in which the Holy Spirit puts us into communion with Christ;
> — in prayer, wherein he intercedes for us;

— in the charisms and ministries by which the Church is built up;
— in the signs of apostolic and missionary life;
— in the witness of saints through whom he manifests his holiness and continues the work of salvation.

— CCC, 688

The Holy Spirit is ever at work, inspiring, guiding, and enabling the Church by His gifts and graces to carry out her mission of evangelization. We can see this especially in the saintly lives and notable accomplishments of men and women who can truly be called "prophets of our times." Chosen by God the Father to bring greater honor and glory to His Incarnate Divine Son, Jesus Christ, and to further the saving and sanctifying work of the Church, they are empowered by the Holy Spirit to proclaim the Gospel message clearly in today's society.

The role of a prophet was never easy. It required a dual faithfulness: both to God and to man! To God, because it was His message the prophets had to proclaim. Therefore, the prophets knew they had to give "the truth, the whole truth, and nothing but the truth" of God's Word when they preached. To man, because the prophets realized that, difficult as the message may sound, the people needed to hear it to bring about their conversion, like taking terrible-tasting medicine as the only remedy for a serious illness.

Often their message was a countercultural value or judgment, guaranteed to bring on resentment, rejection, and even persecution. This is evident when we read about the experiences of the Old Testament prophets. For example, Amaziah, the priest in charge of the royal sanctuary of Bethel, rejected the prophet Amos and told him to leave the Northern Kingdom (called Israel) and return to the Southern Kingdom (called Judah) because he had denounced the Northern Kingdom for its sins of idolatry and injustice (cf. Amos 7:10-17). Likewise, the great prophet Elijah incurred the scorn and wrath of King Ahab and his evil wife, Jezebel, for defeating and destroying the false prophets of the cult of Baal; as a result, he had to flee for his life (cf. 1 Kings 18-19). Perhaps Jeremiah, another great prophet, summed it up best when he wrote:

> O Lord, thou hast deceived me, / and I was deceived; / thou art stronger than I, / and thou hast prevailed. / I have become a laughingstock all the day; / every one mocks me. / For whenever I speak, I cry out, / I shout, "Violence and destruction!" / For the word of the Lord has become for me / a reproach and derision all day long. / If I say, "I will not mention him, / or speak any more in his name," / there is in my heart as it were a burning fire / shut up in my bones, / and I am weary with holding it in, / and I cannot.
>
> — Jeremiah 20:7-9

These words reveal the real anguish and emotion in the heart of Jeremiah! He goes on to acknowledge that he has lost his friends — in fact, they are now his enemies watching his every step to catch him in something they can accuse him of. But he has no fear. Why not? Because the Lord is with him, like a mighty champion to deliver him (cf. Jeremiah 20:10-11).

The Holy Spirit still speaks through the prophets of today. Their words carry His power, a power that convicts the world of her sins of disbelief and immorality (cf. John 16:7-15). Furthermore, their actions are speaking even louder than their words. People from every walk of life, in circumstances favorable and unfavorable to the practice of the Catholic Faith, are crying out the Gospel with their lives, even to the ultimate prophetic witness of dying for Jesus and for their Faith.

In this present time, then, when Pope John Paul II has been God's instrument to call all Christian believers to a "new evangelization," let us ask the Spirit of God to raise up great men and women as "prophets of the Most High." Like St. John the Baptist, who was filled with the Holy Spirit from his mother Elizabeth's womb (cf. Luke 1:39-45), may they — and we, too — speak out courageously the truth of the Christian message of life, love, and peace!

# APPENDIX

# Prayers to the Holy Spirit

## *Veni, Sancte Spiritus* ("Come, Holy Spirit")

Holy Spirit, Lord of Life,
From your clear celestial height
Your pure beaming radiance give.

Come, O Father of the poor;
Come, with treasures that endure;
Come, O light of all who live.

You of all consolers best,
Visiting the troubled breast,
True refreshing peace bestow.

You in toil our comfort sweet,
Pleasant coolness in the heat,
Solace in the midst of woe.

Light immortal, Light divine,
Visit now these hearts of thine
And our inmost being fill.

If you take your grace away,
Nothing pure in us will stay;
All our good is turned to ill.

Heal our wounds, our strength renew;
On our dryness, pour your dew:
Wash the stains of guilt away.

Bend the stubborn heart and will;
Melt the frozen, warm the chill;
Guide the steps that go astray.

You, on those who evermore
Confess you and still adore,
In your sevenfold gifts descend.

Give them comfort when they die,
Give them life with you on high;
Give them joys that never end.
Amen.

### *Veni, Creator Spiritus*
### ("Come, Creator Spirit")

Come, Spirit Creator,
    come live in our minds
    and fill our hearts which you have
        made,
    with perfect grace.

We know you as the Paraclete,
    the gift of God most high,
    our fire, our love, the living fountain
    and holy anointing of our lives.

With seven gifts you act as
    the finger of the Father's right hand;
    you are his promised One,
    teaching us heavenly speech and
        understanding.

Kindle us with fire brought from above,
    pour love into our hearts,
    and give strength
    to our weakness of body.

Drive Satan far away from us,
and give us lasting peace
so that, led by your guidance,
no harm will come to us.

Let us know the Father, through you.
Let us know the Son, through you.
Let us believe forever that you are
the Spirit proceeding from
the Father and the Son.

Glory to the Father,
and glory to his Son,
who rose from death;
and glory to you, kind Strengthener,
for ever and ever.
Amen.

# ABOUT THE AUTHOR

Although Father Andrew J. Apostoli has a number of books to his credit, this is his first for Our Sunday Visitor; his previous books were published by Alba House and the Daughters of St. Paul. He also writes regularly for the magazines *Envoy* and *Soul,* with his column "Food for the Soul" appearing in *Envoy*.

The author hopes that this book of reflections will help readers become more aware of the Holy Spirit at work in their daily Christian life and that it will stimulate meditation on and prayer to the Third Person of the Blessed Trinity.

Father Andrew is a member of the community of the Franciscan Friars of the Renewal. Ordained by Bishop Fulton J. Sheen in 1967, he has been active in teaching, preaching retreats and parish missions, and in giving spiritual direction.